Simply Country Gardens

by Judy Condon

Library of Congress Cataloging-in-Publications Data
Simply Country Gardens by Judy Condon
ISBN 978-0-9843332-3-3

Oceanic Graphic Printing, Inc.
105 Main Street
Hackensack, NJ 07601

Printed in China

Layout and Design by Pat Lucas
Edited by Trent Michaels

About the Author

Judy Condon is a native New Englander, which is evident in her decorating style and the type of antiques she collects and sells. Her real passion is 19thC authentic dry red or blue painted pieces. While July's professional career was as a teacher, Principal and Superintendent of Schools in Connecticut, Judy's weekends were spent at her antique shop, Marsh Homestead Country Antiques, located in Litchfield, Connecticut.

When her husband, Jeff, was relocated to Virginia, Judy accepted an early retirement from education and concentrated her energy and passion for antiques into a fulltime business. Judy maintains a website, http//www.marshhomesteadantiques.com and has been a Power Seller on eBay® for over twelve years under the name "superct".

With the success of her books and her working relationships with country shops throughout the United States and Canada, Judy created a successful wholesale business featuring hand-poured primitive wax pieces and other handmade country accessories that she sold to shops. Judy's time is not taken up solely with the "simply country" books.

Judy has five children and five grandchildren and lives in Spotsylvania, Virginia with her husband Jeff.

Judy's first thirteen books in the "simply country" series have been instant hits and many in their second printing. Judy may be reached through her website, her email address, marshhomestead@comcast.net or 877-381-6682

Introduction

My husband, Jeff, often laughs when I refer to myself as "a war baby". My father was stationed in the South Pacific during WWII and didn't lay eyes on me until I was two-and-a-half. My mother and I lived with her parents on Long Island Sound in Connecticut. Because my father was away at war, my mother created an extensive photographic history of my early life to share with him … so my early years are well documented.

My grandmother operated a baking business from their home, and my childhood memories recall her 4'10" frame bustling around her kitchen preparing either 150 pot pies for someone's wedding, or the cake itself for the bride and groom.

When she was not busy in her kitchen or pantry, she spent time in her gardens. Her flower beds were huge! Extensive! They stretched from the front porch 100 yards down either side of the lawn, ending at the seawall of the Sound. In the center were four large beds of rose bushes surrounding a small goldfish pond. (We didn't know about koi back then).

I watched my grandmother care for her flower beds for years. She showed me how a snapdragon got its name when the flower was gently squeezed, and all about, "She loves me, she loves me not", when plucking daisy petals. My job as a young girl involved removing the Japanese beetles from the rose bushes and dropping them in a tin can filled with kerosene. I remember feeling quite important because, even as a little girl, I was entrusted with this awesome responsibility; my grandmother knew that I would tread lightly through the rose beds to perform my task.

My grandmother instilled in me the love of gardening and the beauty of flowers. Simple daisies remain my favorite, yet I don't pass a rose without thinking of the bouquets placed throughout my grandmother's home.

Table of Contents

The Apple Gardens

North Carolina

like
Chair

like
need flag

The Barnes Gardens

Georgia

The Coffin Gardens
Illinois

like inside

The Crane Gardens

Illinois

like clematis

need a wagon

like bunny

Bird houses —
fence —

The DeYoung Gardens
Massachusetts

like

The Foster Gardens

Delaware

The Freed Gardens
Massachusetts

The Graybill Gardens

Pennsylvania

The Harris Gardens

New York

The Helbig Gardens

Massachusetts

The Hinson Gardens

North Carolina

The Lang Gardens

New Hampshire

PICK YOUR OWN FLOWERS

The Lezu Gardens
North Carolina

The Litwin Gardens
Connecticut

The Mills Gardens

Illinois

The Morello Gardens

Massachusetts

Like sidewalk ↓

Like ↘

Like ↑

The Paulin Gardens

Maine

The Pollack Gardens
South Carolina

Like Boots

The St. Mark Gardens
Connecticut

The Walker Gardens
Illinois

The Weaver Gardens
Ohio

The Wolff Gardens

Connecticut

Our Contributors

Jo Apple

Now that Jo has retired from a job which required her to travel for seven years from Monday morning until Thursday night, she is thoroughly enjoying the twelve acres she owns and maintains. In 1981, Jo decided to build a log cabin, something her ailing father would enjoy watching take shape, and someplace she could stay on weekends when providing care for her dad. In 1996, Jo moved permanently to the log cabin and added a large addition to accommodate year-round living. Jo's grandparents were avid gardeners, and when they sold their home, Jo was able to rescue numerous bulbs and plantings, which now hold special meaning for Jo. Over the years, numerous trees had fallen on the property and a friend offered to clean up the dead trees, a job which took four months to complete. Huge piles of wood chip mulch and worn-down paths remained where tractors and other equipment had crisscrossed to clear the woods. Although the paths through Jo's property look planned, she admits she simply spread the mulch over the one-and-a-half miles of paths. Since then, Jo added bridges and rocks to channel runoff water into creek beds. Jo had the trails covered with sand rock, which makes them more durable; she maintains the trails by raking them faithfully every three months.

Janie and Brad Barnes

Janie and Brad met on a blind date in college 37 years ago. Janie grew up in a small town in North Carolina which was, at that time, the largest tobacco-growing area in the world. As a result, she says she grew up on "tobacco road". When Brad and Janie first married they lived close enough to Williamsburg, Virginia for Janie to become intrigued with the colonial style of decorating typical of Williamsburg, yet unwilling to give up her love for American country. Her gardens reflect her interest in the Williamsburg style and are filled with a large variety of herbs. While the herb garden is uniform, Janie demonstrates her love of country style decorating by the random scattering of birdhouses and other country garden ornaments over the rest of her gardens. Of particular interest is the native North Carolina evergreen vine called Smilax over the front door. For years while on the way to work, Janie passed a home draped with Smilax. Coincidentally, Janie learned that the owner of the home was a woman by the name of Dot Eagles, who attended the same church as Janie and Brad. Months later, when Brad and Janie were moving, Janie was returning home from work when Dot flagged her down and insisted that Janie, despite being dressed in heels and work attire, help dig up the baby Smilax and take it as a gift. Janie has moved the plant she now refers to as Miss Dot to four houses, where it continues to thrive and serves as a reminder of a woman Janie greatly admired and wishes to emulate.

Jody and J.J. Coffin

J.J. and Jody Coffin's home was featured in an earlier book, *The Comfort of Home*, but their gardens are so extensive that I wanted to feature them in *Simply Country Gardens* as well. J.J. built both log buildings in their gardens; the log building shown on the cover was reconstructed with logs from a cabin in Madison, Indiana. Jody has never amended her soil and shared that a nearby location reportedly features the richest soil in the world. Jody deadheads daily to keep the gardens fresh and finds that a product called Preen, which she spreads when planting, helps keep the weeds at bay. A few years ago, Jody planted approximately one hundred perennials, which the garden center told her she would live to regret. She hasn't and claims to have added many more since. J.J. and Jody combine their creative talents in their home and their business. Jody and J.J. design beautiful country calendars, note cards, and most recently, the best rush lights from old materials which look absolutely authentic. Some of them were seen in the house tour book *The Comfort of Home*. J.J. and Jody may be reached by phone at 217-892-4078 or email at *squarenailjjjc@mchsi.com*.

Gary and Marsa Crane

When Gary and Marsa moved into their home twenty years ago, there were two spruce trees in the front yard and that was it. Marsa views the trees in her yard as the "bones" to her garden; she is careful to select trees which will remain green throughout the winter and continue to provide a backdrop for her garden "hardware" despite the lack of flowers and color. Marsa favors a garden with many textures and one that incorporates nature. She believes that nothing should be straight in a garden; the stones should be random and the flag stone paths meandering. Marsa is the first to admit that her garden has evolved over the years. She began with one vignette, much as we do when we decorate a home. Now her garden consists of a number of "rooms", such as the cozy area in the backyard where her granddaughters have tea parties on the overturned galvanized tub. While the shed started out as a potting shed, it too has evolved into an area shared with granddaughters, who dress in fancy hats as they build memories with their grandparents. A lovely full-size stained glass window casts lovely light on the nearby area. Marsa enjoys plantings which provide color throughout the seasons and enjoys changing plants in an area much as we redecorate our homes when a new treasure is discovered. Gary enjoys working in the garden as well and particularly enjoys growing sunflowers, the tallest of which last summer reached 18 feet.

Janet and Glenn DeYoung

Glenn and Janet DeYoung live in a reproduction Sturbridge Village style home and adamantly declare every year that they will not add to their garden because they don't want all the work! Each year they say the same thing and each year their gardens evolve into something bigger and better than the year before. Their gardens are a labor of love and a team effort. John works as a property manager for homes housing handicapped individuals, but finds the time to cut, water, and convert wooded areas into new flower beds. Janet, a retired teacher, works part time in the local educational system but still manages to find endless hours in the summer to devote to her gardens. One of the whimsical highlights in their garden is an actual-size outhouse built to conceal a large, unsightly propane gas tank! I also loved the idea of using andirons in the garden to hold a flower-filled galvanized tub. The DeYoung's home will be featured in another "simply country" book in 2012. Thanks to the DeYoung's niece Lisa Diotte, for her photographic contributions.

Susan and Bob Foster

Twenty-six years ago, Susan and Bob Foster bought their 1980's home in Delaware. Susan replaced the shrubs against the foundation with rose bushes and other typical "suburban" plants. That was before she started to work as a greenhouse technician at the University of Delaware. Susan took classes in plant science such as Plant Physiology and Native Wildflowers and began to rethink her garden in favor of native plants. Susan's gardens are now 95% native and include trillium species and native orchids, to name a few. Susan has created a habitat conducive to regular visitors such as red-tailed hawks, nesting peregrine falcons, and numerous song birds. Susan is in the process of completing her PhD in agriculture. As a Master Gardener, Susan highly recommends a book titled *Bringing Nature Home* by Dr. Doug Tallamy. The book is a culmination of 20 years of research regarding the need for additional native habitats in suburban gardens to help reverse the loss of native fauna, specifically insects.

Dianne and Ken Freed

Dianne and Ken Freed live in Rehoboth, Massachusetts, in the Thomas Carpenter home built in 1789. Originally, the Carpenter home was a 100 acre farmstead that remained in the same family for over 100 years. Since 1900, the property has served as a dairy farm and a rural retreat; gradually parcels were sold for development. Presently the property consists of two-and-a-half acres; a number of families have enjoyed this special home. When Dianne and Ken are not working in their gardens, they participate in antique shows in New England. They once owned a country antique shop for twelve years; now Dianne and Ken maintain a Website business, *New England Seasons*, which features a diverse selection of antiques and reproduction accessories. Their Website can be accessed at *www.newenglandseasons.com*. Dianne and Ken also rent space at Enchanted Yesteryears in North Scituate, Rhode Island.

Georgie and John Graybill

Georgie and John Graybill have lived in their Macungie, Pennsylvania stone house for the past 31 years. Their home was built in 1820 and will be featured in a 2012 "simply country" book. I guarantee the reader will be delighted with the interior decorating and warmth of their home. The log shed in the back garden was purchased from Ginny Curry Antiques in Ohio and moved, via a rented truck, by John and Georgie to their yard, where John reconstructed the building. Georgie likes to decorate her garden with whimsical pieces; she displays her collection of early rotary hoe wheels on the fence. Pots with early pulleys and chains hold flowers around the patio area. An early yoke in the garden holds more pots with annual flowers. After reading an article in Early American Life covering the early art of espalier; a pruning technique with fruit trees to train and control their growth. Georgie planted a Macintosh apple tree against the back wall of her garden and is training it to grow while supported by metal rods.

Martha and Robert Harris

Robert and Martha Harris moved from Long Island to Upstate New York and are bound and determined to create a farm. While Robert is retired and enjoys painting when not working in the garden, Martha is still employed as a second-grade teacher. In their spare time, they raise chickens and grow all their own vegetables. Two years ago they started a candle-making business called *Farmstead Candles* and sell their products from their home and wholesale to shops in the area. Their candles are poured into mason jars and made from natural soy. For more information, Robert and Martha may be reached at 315-685-2077 or email *mj.theoharis@gmail.com*.

Jo-Ann and John Helbig

In the 1990's, John and Jo-Ann offered to move back to her 1790's childhood home in Leyden, Massachusetts to take care of her elderly father. After working three months restoring the old home, John and Jo-Ann sold their A-frame next door and Jo-Ann became her family's fourth generation to live in the house. When Jo-Ann isn't making dolls (she was listed last year in the Early American Craft Directory for her interpretation of early dolls), she particularly enjoys gardening and collecting primitives. Although John is still employed at a nearby paper mill, he helps Jo-Ann with her antique business and shows. Jo-Ann does the Brimfield Show in Massachusetts three times a year. Also, periodically throughout the year, Jo-Ann fills the outbuildings, which John built for her, with antiques and conducts open houses. John and Jo-Ann breed and raise West Highland white terriers for use as therapy dogs. The dogs participate in an eight-week training course and then are registered to visit area nursing homes and provide therapeutic comfort to the elderly. For information on Jo-Ann's open house schedule, please contact her at 413-773-5349.

Sherrie and Ernie Hinson

Sherrie, a South Carolina native, grew up on a farm and has combined her love of primitives and gardening by surrounding her 1987 Low Country-style home with whimsical gardens. Sherrie and Ernie enjoy mixing old pieces such as beds, toys, broken salt-glazed pottery, and farm tools in their gardens; they don't hesitate to stop along the road and pick up a discarded article. Sherrie loves to let her imagination run wild but is careful not to let it get out of hand. Sherrie has spend the last few years caregiving an elderly parent and finds gardening therapeutic for relieving stress. Sherrie mows her lawn twice a week and uses the time to relax and think. Her neighbors used to stop and question why she was mowing the lawn again and now just stop and say, "I see you're doing some thinking." Sherrie cares for two grandchildren, aged five and three, and is thrilled that they have each taken to her garden and enjoy learning how to care for it. Sherrie maintains booth space at the Golden Leaf Antique Mall in Mullins, South Carolina, which is housed in an old tobacco warehouse. She creates and sells note cards under her business name, *Simpler Times*, and also sells bunches of tallow berries known as Charleston Popcorn, which she grows in her yard. Sherri may be reached via email at *sherrie7200@att.net*.

Karen and Dave Lang

Karen's garden is a living memorial to her mom. Karen and Dave Lang had always lived next door to Karen's mom, June, an avid gardener. Karen reports that her mom designed and planted the garden and tended it throughout the year. June passed away last year after a long illness, and Karen is trying to pick up the maintenance of her gardens where June left off. "June's gardens" are visible from every window of Karen and Dave's home and, according to Karen, a day doesn't go by when Karen looks out the window and does not enjoy seeing June's handiwork. Last summer, Dave and Karen added a stone garden bench, also visible from each window, in memory of Karen's mom and the lifelong joy she has left to Karen and her family. At the back of the wooded property, a visitor follows a path lined with shade plants over a bridge which fords a trickling brook. Here, Dave built a "summer cottage" as a summer evening escape.

Alice and Michael Lezu

Alice and Michael Lezu have lived in their 1980 reproduction colonial in Claremont, New Hampshire for two years—which means it's about time for them to move! They love to move and have done so 17 times. Michael is a manager at K-Mart which affords them the opportunity to just pack up and start again. Their amazing home will be featured in 2012 in a "simply country" house tour book. Michael and Alice are both Master Gardeners with very dissimilar styles and, as a result, a visitor can easily discern which area of the yard each maintains. Michael prefers everything in its place and designs open ground around his plants. He built the edging on either side of the stairway leading down to the backyard and also created the structured circular garden in the front yard. Alice, on the other hand, likes to see established gardens full of flowers with one plant taking over the next. They agree, though, that the secret to successful gardens is to dig out an area using fresh soil and compost. Michael uses bark mulch around his plants while Alice simply aerates the soil. If you were a gardener, wouldn't you love to buy their house when it goes on the market?

Eileen and Peter Litwin

Peter Litwin, a retired attorney and his wife Eileen, a retired physical therapist, live in the house called Arbutus Farm where Peter grew up in Litchfield, Connecticut. Peter and Eileen's magnificent home, featured in a "simply country" series book available in 2012, reflects the eclectic mix of Peter's passion for folk art, nature, and art. Peter's love of stone is reflected in the unique and tasteful placement of various pieces throughout the property– from the large cascading stone step fountain to the patio table created with an early grinding stone. Peter researched the effect of tilting a garden 10 degrees toward the sun, and learned that the incline duplicated the sunlight of climate 300 miles further south. For that reason, Peter built up the three walls on the north slope to tilt the garden and believes it has made a huge difference in its productivity. Peter is a master craftsman (which he would never admit) and has created a collection of small carved birds. He also builds furniture and fashions burl bowls.

Brenda and Dan Mills

When Brenda first married and had young children, she viewed gardening as keeping a few flower pots on the steps. Then she met a farmer's wife who invited her to visit her place a few miles down the road. What Brenda found behind the woman's house were magnificent gardens, and Brenda decided she could do that! Starting with a little section of her yard, Brenda began to build what she calls little "rooms" of plants and flowers. Now, fifteen years later, the Mills' yard is a glorious oasis surrounded by cornfields. Brenda does not intend to expand her gardens; she recognizes that in a few years she will not wish to maintain the space she already has. She does, however, change and rearrange plants constantly. One garden piece that holds sentimental value is a bench in the front area which she purchased with a small inheritance from an uncle. She refers to the bench as the Hubbard bench and enjoys it as a reminder of her family. The shed in the back also holds special meaning to Dan and Brenda. Dan raised hogs for a time, and when dismantling the farm he decided to save the wood and tin roof from the barn for use someday. Dan built the shed as a birthday gift to Brenda, incorporating an old workbench belonging to Dan's grandfather as the potting stand. Brenda likes to use rocks in her garden, but in Illinois they're difficult to find. Dan and Brenda have made two trips to northern Indiana to bring back a truckload of rocks to pile in her garden. One pile rests beside the stack of early grinding wheels which Brenda and Dan made into a fountain.

Ruth and Bill Walker

Ruth's garden is a perfect example of the beauty and serenity which can be achieved in a shaded area. Ruth, a Master Gardener, also belongs to the Hosta Society, a national organization which meets annually to share gardening ideas. Ruth believes her love of gardening comes from her father; she remembers watching him deadhead the garden each fall with a lawn mower. Ruth is a bit more methodical than her dad. As a matter of fact, in the spring, her front lawn (originally a pasture) fills with tiny white flowers, and Ruth and Bill refuse to mow their lawn for a month. Champaign County in Illinois reportedly has some of the richest soil in the country, which perhaps explains why the area grows corn and soy beans so abundantly. When Bill and Ruth first moved into their home, their property was completely wooded; they immediately began to cut down over 200 trees, leaving only enough to provide the shade they enjoy today. Ruth particularly enjoys her trillium, jack-in-the-pulpits, and numerous varieties of ferns. Ruth is happy to speak with anyone who likes to talk or ask about gardens. As she said, "I've never met a gardener I didn't like." Ruth can be reached at 217-649-6918.

Sue Morello

Sue acquired her love of antiques from her father, who operated an antique shop in Salem, Massachusetts for many years. Sue bought the property she named Sheldon Farm 14 years ago at auction. In addition to restoring the house, which will be seen in a "simply country" holiday book in 2011, Sue focused attention on landscaping the property. Richie Hayse of Stonewall Restorations built the stone walls, patio, and stone gardens. Sue spends endless hours maintaining her gardens now that she is retired. Sue, a member of the Spencer Garden Club, uses primarily perennials and expands her garden space each year. Sue also makes baskets and sells from the Website her son Mikal created for her as a retirement gift. For more information on Sue's baskets or to place an order, please visit Sue's Website at *www.sheldonfarmbaskets.com*. Thanks to Mikal and his friend Cole Hubacz for their photographic contributions.

Chris and Mavis Newton

Mavis, an Iowa native, grew up on a farm where her dad planted soy beans and corn. Her job was to walk the fields and pick up rocks; her sister was the tomboy who enjoyed the farm. Chris, a Missouri native, lived on an Amish farm during his college years and perhaps that's where it all started. When Mavis married Chris 10 years ago, she knew she was marrying a hospital administrator and thought she would live in a sub-division and raise a family. Chris worked at a VA hospital in Rhode Island while Mavis pursued her career as a teacher. One day Chris decided he wanted a family cow, which cannot be raised on a three-quarter acre parcel. So they began looking for a farm. Chris and Mavis found the farm of their dreams in Canterbury, Connecticut, a 1982 replica home of an Old Sturbridge Village home. One cow led to two, then three, which Chris milked twice a day in addition to his regular job. When the workload became too much, Chris and Mavis decided to automate- which meant to be profitable they needed to purchase more cows. After procuring a license, Mavis now oversees and supervises Baldwin Brook Dairy which sells non-pasteurized and non homogenized milk to retailers and cheese makers.

Their livestock now includes a flock of two hundred chickens, beef cattle, pigs, ducks, and rabbits. They employ six part-time employees, operating an onsite store where they sell raw milk, grass fed beef, eggs, pasteurized pork, and honey. Mavis also conducts mini-tours and demonstrations for small groups of children when she is not working in the gorgeous gardens leading up to and surrounding the property. Oh…. I forgot to mention their son Clay who was born 18 months ago! And also, along the way they met and befriended Phyllis, who in fact lived on her family farm and was caregiving an elderly parent. Chris and Mavis invited "Aunt" Phyllis to come live with them after her parent passed. So Phyllis built a home attached to Chris and Mavis' and helps with the store and childcare.

For store hours and information, please call Chris and Mavis of *Baldwin Brook Farm* at 860-546-2137 or by email *cmnewt@sbcglobal.net*.

Debbie and Guy Paulin

Debbie and Guy Paulin of Limington, Maine built their Cape style home themselves and maintain the surrounding grounds. Debbie owns a shop on the property called *The Country Collection*, which is open from May-December, Thursday–Sunday. They combined their talents to create a successful business; Guy designs and creates unique pieces in his workshop for Debbie to display and sell. Customers anxiously await the annual building Guy creates for the holidays to add to their village collection. Guy is currently creating birdhouses similar to the one shown in this chapter. Guy also built the stone mushroom fountains which can be seen in the patio area of their garden.

Guy and Debbie also help with the apple orchard and blueberry fields located on the adjoining property belonging to Debbie's father. Guy's artistic abilities were featured in the second book in the "simply country" series, *Of Hearth and Home*; the mural featured on the cover was painted by Guy. Guy and Debbie can be reached at 207-637-2580 or by email through their Website *www.thecountrycollection.net*.

Mary Ann and Alan Pollack

Although Mary Ann wouldn't admit it, I would consider her to be a master gardener who last year won the Garden of the Month award from the Quail Valley Garden Club. Now retired as a real estate broker, she works in her gardens the better part of each day. Mary Ann attributes her love of gardening to her mother; she remembers her mother's side border gardens and watching her mother faithfully water them each night. Mary Ann doesn't hesitate to replant or remove plants on a regular basis to either accommodate new plants or take advantage of lighting or groupings by size or color. Her favorite plant is the English heather.

Mary Ann and a partner maintain a country shop called *The Primitive Crow* in Columbia, South Carolina. She also operates a felting wool business whereby she washes 100% wool in hot water and dries it–a process called felting; Mary Ann sells the thicker woven finished felt to the public for craft projects. She sells her felt on a Website designed for the sale of handmade pieces or products called Etsy under the ID WoolenCrow. She may also be reached by phone at 803-467-5511.

Carole St. Mark

Carole, formerly an executive for a large, Connecticut-based company, purchases her mulch not by the bag but by the pallet–four pallets per year. Acres of cultivated gardens surround her 18thC magnificently restored farmhouse, which will be featured in a forthcoming "simply country" book. Each area of the garden features its own vignette–some ornate and others simplified with only the beauty of color. When not working in her gardens or selling select antiques on Ebay® under the ID coasterpatrick, Carole owns and manages *Far Meadow Farm*, a full service horse stable and training facility in Morris, Connecticut. For information, please access her Website: *www.farmeadowfarm.com*. Thanks to Elizabeth Wue for her photographic contributions.

Tammy and Vic Weaver

Tammy and Vic purchased their 1830's farmhouse in Millersburg, Ohio from her brother; the house had been in Tammy's family for generations. The farmhouse will be featured in a 2012 "simply country" house tour book. Tammy loves to add old structural pieces to her gardens such as pillars and fountains. She also utilizes running water wherever possible and loves its peaceful sound. One of Tammy's fountains was crafted from a water trough that she recalls was used by horses when she was a child. Many of the flowers in Tammy's garden have come from friends, and anytime she moved prior to purchasing the farmhouse, she was careful to take the plants with her. Most of all she relishes those heirloom plants which belonged to her grandmother.

Tammy is a buyer and manager at *Country Gatherings*, part of the *Berlin Gift Shop* located in nearby Berlin, Ohio. The small gardens planted in metal tubs, sometimes referred to as "fairy gardens", are sold at *Country Gatherings*. Vic rebuilt the potting shed on the property for Tammy as a gift; it had previously been used as their daughter's childhood playhouse. Tammy loves to use Americana accessories in her gardens; she added a large flag in front of the shed and smaller ones in surrounding beds.

Guy Wolff and Erica Warnock

Guy Wolff, a professional potter since 1971, operates his business, *Wolff Pottery*, from his workshop in Litchfield, Connecticut. Guy sells his pottery to shops, botanical gardens, museums, and privately to individuals. His designs have been distributed nationally, appearing in many publications including Martha Stewart Living Magazine and a special edition of Better Homes and Gardens. Erica, who helps create small pots, is a musician who plays early chamber music on an instrument called a viola da camba at concerts in Connecticut and New York. Guy Wolff may be reached at *Guy Wolff Pottery*, PO Box 868, Litchfield, Connecticut, by phone at 860-567-5577, or his Website *www.Wolffpottery.com*.

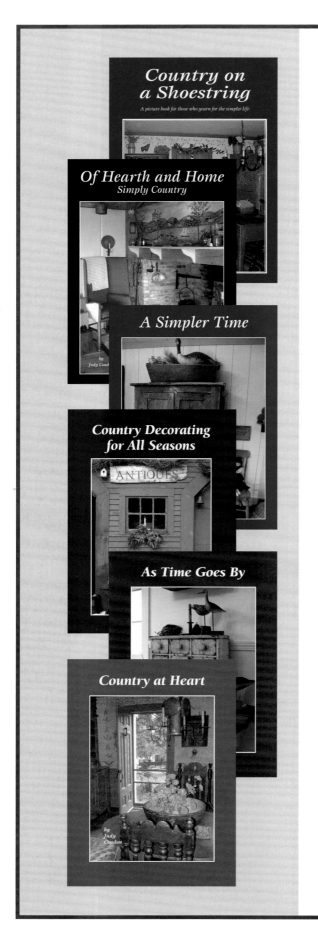

The "simply country" book series

by Judy Condon

Country on a Shoestring
- 33 tips on how to decorate on a shoestring

Of Hearth and Home
- mantels, old painted pieces, signs and primitives

A Simpler Time
- log homes, bedrooms, kitchens, dining rooms, folk art and stencils

Country Decorating for All Seasons
- holiday doors, porches, mantels, trees, vignettes; summer gardens, and fall decorating

As Time Goes By
- The Keeping Room; boxes, baskets and bowls; The Privy; Hallways and Small Ways; The Guest Room

Country at Heart
- The Tavern Room; early looms, dolls and bears; The Gathering Room; a kitchen aged to perfection; country gardens

Welcome Home
- New house tour format; 2 Connecticut homes and 5 Ohio Homes; plus a never before photographed Shaker collection

Home Again
- 7 Ohio homes, 1 Maine home

The Warmth of Home
- 3 Massachusetts homes, 1 Pennsylvania home, 3 Ohio homes, 1 New York home and 1 Delaware home

The Country Home

- 6 Ohio homes, 2 Massachusetts homes, 1 New Hampshire home

The Comfort of Home

- Over 325 color photographs showing a Massachusetts and Ohio home of two exceptional collectors. A Maine home; three Massachusetts homes, one of which is in the city; a New Hampshire home decorated in "first period".

Simple Greens – Simply Country

- Over 400 color photographs of country homes decorated for the holidays. Also a chapter on "how to make a country bed" and the recipe for the large decorative gingerbread boys and pantry cakes.

The Country Life

- The homes of four antique dealers will be featured in this book; Marjorie Staufer of Ohio, Colette Donovan, Molly Garland and Kathy Hopper all of Massachusetts. Also included will be the home of Robin and Bill Campanale showing rooms of early painted pieces; the home of Kathy Spellacy of Maine; the decorated first period home of Adam and Mary Spencer of New Hampshire; the home of Shelly Leclair in Massachusetts and that of children's book author Mark Kimball Moulton.

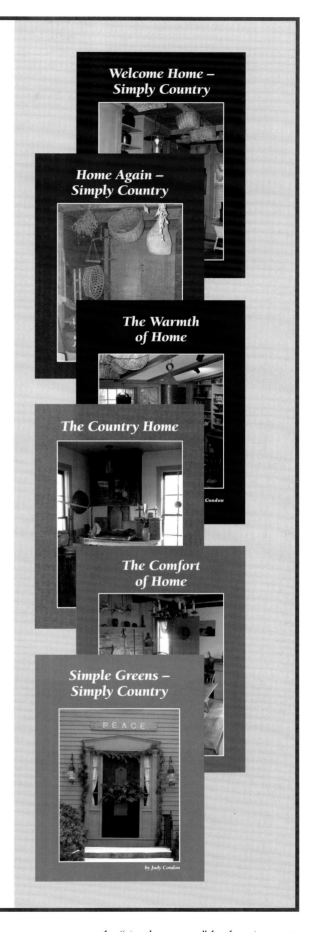

As the weary months of cold winter weather draw to a close, I relish pouring through garden books in anticipation of spring and the emergence of my flowers. With winter past, spring embodies all that is relevant to the future: the reappearance of sunlight, warmth, and new life. I plant perennials almost exclusively, as they represent my faith in the potential of the future and the excitement of welcoming old friends back in my garden.

We lovers of country have found the means to integrate our country pieces into our gardens and bring our indoor and outdoor decorating together. A simple, rusty form adds beauty to our landscape or enhances a flower bed and, to my eye, contributes to the beauty and sense of peace in *Simply Country Gardens*.

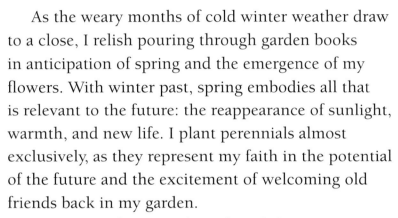